Handstand

Organic Soy Sauce 10 FL. OZ

Chinese Cookbook
By Yvette Garfield
Illustrated by Kim DeRose
Recipes by Shanti Jade Greenspan

Published by Handstand Kids, LLC

Printed In China by Amica Inc., March 28, 2011

ISBN: 978-0-9792107-4-7

By Yvette Garfield

Illustrated by Kim DeRose

Designed by Vani Sodhi Gundara

Recipes Edited and Developed by Shanti Jade Greenspan

Editing by Tracy Sway

Translations by Grace Lin

This Book Belongs To:

2

Dedication

This book is dedicated to Arlene and Marvin Garfield, who continue to inspire me in every facet of my life and teach me to find the humor in even the most challenging times.

Special Thanks

Many thanks to Kim DeRose, Shanti Greenspan, Tracy Sway and Vani Gundara for making my third cookbook the most fun and enjoyable to create! Your talent and passion continue to impress and motivate me.

To Alix, Ana, Ariel, Gaea, Hannah, Jenn, Kim, Liz, Liza, Rebecca, Shana, Shanti, Smriti, Tracy and Valerie for being my source of strength and teaching me what girl power is!

Table of Contents

Foreword by Ming Tsai
Executive Producer of Simply Ming
CHEF/OWNER of Blue Ginger

In Chinese culture, the common greeting is **Chi le ma**. This does not translate to "Hello" or "How are you?" but "Have you eaten?" That's how important food is in Chinese culture! I am proud to be Chinese-American and so grateful that I grew up eating some of the best food in the world. Chinese civilization has been around for centuries—we've had time to perfect our cooking!

Most of my favorite memories from childhood involve food, and that's not just because I love to eat. I love recalling the afternoons I spent picking the tiny hairs off bean sprouts while my aunts and grandmother bustled about the kitchen cooking the family's meal. It was a time to tell stories, learn new things, and just be in each other's company. As I grew older, the tasks changed, and I learned tricks and techniques I still use today—tricks like how to roll a spring roll, the best way to pleat dumplings, and how to calculate the correct amount of water for making rice without using a measuring cup.

Becoming involved in creating our family's meals provided me with wonderful memories and great cooking skills, but it also helped me appreciate food. Watching my grandfather relish every bite of the baby bok choy stir-fry that I helped prepare filled me with pride, and also made me want to try a bite, even if it hadn't appealed to me when I was helping to wash the grit out of that bok choy earlier in the day (there is nothing worse than grit in your bok choy!). Trying foods other people enjoy gives you the chance to enjoy new foods you may not have tasted before. Cooking and sharing food together is also a great way to spend time with someone you love. When you cook for someone, you show them you care, and when you sit down to a meal with friends or family, you are spending some very special time with them.

Food plays a very important role in almost every culture. Many holidays and family gatherings revolve around eating and cooking. Food is the great common denominator—it connects all of us. For example, everybody has a favorite food—what is yours? As you learn about the different foods from various cultures, you'll learn what separates us and what connects us. For example, a pot sticker in Chinese cuisine is very similar to the pierogi from Polish cuisine, which is also much like Italy's ravioli. And so on, and so on!

In my family, when we sit down at the table, we often **say qing-chi—please dine!** I hope you have a fantastic time creating recipes from the Handstand Kids Chinese Cookbook; learn from it, experiment with it, make fantastic dishes from it and don't forget to say **qing-chi** to your friends and family!

Peace & Good Eating!
Ming Tsai

Utensils
in English and Chinese:

Can Opener

开罐器
Kai guan chi

Cutting Board

砧板
Jen ban

Baking Sheet

烤盘纸
Kao pan zhi

Blender

搅拌机
Jiao ban ji

Bowls
(large, medium and small)

碗（大, 中, 小）
Wan (da, jung, shiau)

Fork

餐叉
Can cha

Knife

刀子
Can dao

Measuring Cup

量杯
Liang bei

Measuring Spoon

量匙
Liang chi

Grater

磨光机
Mo guang ji

Pastry Brush

面饼刷
Mian bing shua

Plate

盘子
Pan zi

Saucepan
(large and small)

平底深锅（大 & 小）
Ping di shen guo
(da & shiau)

Skillet

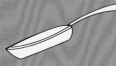

长柄平底煎锅
Chang bing ping
di jian guo

Spatula

刮铲
Gua chan

Spoon

汤匙
Tang chi

Strainer

滤网
Lu wang

Whisk

打蛋器
Da dan chi

Wooden Spoon

木勺
Mu shao

Drinking Glass

玻璃杯
Bo li bei

Wok

铁锅
Tie guo

Ingredients
in English and Chinese:

Bananas

香蕉
shiang jiau

Bell peppers

青椒
Ching jiau

Broth (chicken or vegetable)

清汤
Ching tang

Broccoli

花椰菜
Hua ye tsai

Carrots

胡萝卜
Hu luo bo

Celery

芹菜
Chin tsai

Chicken

鸡
Ji rou

Eggs

蛋
Dan

Garlic

大蒜
Da suan

Ginger

姜
Jiang

Green onions

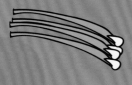

葱
Cong

Honey

蜂蜜
Feng mi

Lettuce

生菜
Wo ju

Mushrooms

香菇
Mo gu

7

Oil

油
Yo

Onion

洋葱
Yang cong

Peanut Butter

花生酱
Hua sheng jiang

Popcorn

爆米花
Bau mi hua

Rice
(brown and white)

米饭

Mi fan

Salt and pepper

盐 胡椒
Yan hu jiau

Shrimp

虾
Shia tz

Snow Peas

雪豆
Shiue dou

Soy sauce

酱油
Jiang yo

Spring roll

春卷
Chun juan

Spring roll wrappers

春卷皮
Chun juan pi

Sugar

糖

Tang

Tofu

豆腐
Dofu

Wontons

馄饨
Hun tun

Recipe Levels: Chopsticks

Look for the chopsticks at the top of each recipe to determine the recipe's level of difficulty. Each recipe is ranked between levels 1 and 4; more chopsticks means that more adult help is encouraged.

Remember, an adult supervisor must be in the kitchen at all times!

1 set of Chopsticks – Level 1 means this is a basic recipe and that you can do most of the steps yourself.

2 sets of Chopsticks – Level 2 means that the recipe is a little bit harder and there are some steps that an adult will need to help you with.

3 sets of Chopsticks – Level 3 means that an adult will need to handle certain steps.

4 sets of Chopsticks – Level 4 means that an adult will need to help you with the entire recipe.

Stir It Up!

Congratulations on becoming a Chinese chef!

Cooking and eating these tasty Chinese dishes is tons of fun, but you can also use your new cooking skills to brighten someone else's day! Try making these recipes for your friends and family.

Your cooking skills can also be used to help those in need. Local charities and food banks may welcome food donations and youth volunteers; check the Handstand Kids website for volunteer opportunities at *www.handstandkids.com*.

Using your new cooking skills in these ways can help change the world, so lets get started!

Introduction

Welcome to the Handstand Kids Chinese Cookbook! Food is a fun and hands-on way to learn about people and cultures around the world. When you learn to cook recipes from another country, you open your kitchen to a world of experiences. While people around the world have many differences, they all have delicious foods and recipes that are special to their region.

The Handstand Kids (Ari, Felix, Gabby, Izzy and Marvin) can't wait to introduce you to Chinese cooking. While making some of China's tastiest and most nutritious recipes, you will be introduced to the Mandarin language, which is spoken throughout China. Soon you will be on your way to becoming a Chinese chef!

Each recipe in this book offers an alternative suggestion that encourages you to add your own favorite flavors and creativity to the recipe.

An adult supervisor must be present in the kitchen at all times to assist kid chefs, especially when cooking over the stove or using sharp objects. Adult supervision will ensure that kid chefs are always safe.

Cooking is a fun, wonderful skill that you can use to help people. Making a special meal for a loved one will make his or her day! Bake sales and food fundraisers are also wonderful ways to raise money for a local group. Many charities allow youth volunteers to help those in need. Check the Handstand Kids website for volunteer opportunities at www.handstandkids.com.

It is my hope that the Handstand Kids cookbook series will provide you with a fun and tasty way to learn about other places and people, and that the Handstand Kids will inspire you to help make the world a better place.

So join the Handstand Kids as they travel the world, one recipe at a time!

Yvette Garfield

Meet The

IZZY

Birthday July 5

Hey! I'm Izzy and I'm 10 ½ years old. Everyone says I am the pickiest eater, but I love spaghetti, so I think I will also like the Chow Mein Long Life Noodles. It will be so fun to make them.

I also really want to make the Year of the Monkey Mango Smoothie for my sister! She is diabetic so she can't eat food with sugar. I think she will love the smoothie and drink it all the time.

FELIX

Birthday February 8

Greetings! I'm Felix and I am nine years old. I love taking cooking classes at my school. I am a vegetarian which means that I don't eat any meat. My whole family is vegetarian so we all love having tofu dishes for holidays. It will be awesome to make the Kung Pow! Tofu for my family to eat.

I also want to learn how to make more after-school snacks for my friends to enjoy with me.

Organic Peanut Butter

Rice Paper

Net Weight 17.6 oz.

Handstand Kids

GABBY

Birthday October 7

Hi! I'm Gabby and I am eleven years old. My favorite hobby is learning new languages. So far I can speak three languages pretty well: English, Spanish and Farsi. I absolutely love learning new words and I hope that one day I can speak to everyone in the world in their native language. I know that's ambitious, but I am starting young.

I am so excited to learn Mandarin. We will learn the characters and how to pronounce the words (phonetics). It will be so cool to make Chinese food with my friends and teach them Mandarin words!

MARVIN

Birthday April 19

Hi! I'm Marvin and I want to be a chef when I grow up. I'm only ten so I still have a lot to learn about cooking. My mom lets me help in the kitchen so I can learn from her. She has traveled all around the world so we cook all different kinds of food. When I was eight, she took me to Italy and I loved eating the pizza. I can't wait to try Chinese Chicken Pizza!

After I go to college, I want to open a restaurant and serve foods from around the world. I will definitely have some Chinese food on the menu!

ARI

Birthday December 17

Hello there. My name is Ari and I am eight years old. I love to eat all kinds of foods! My family thinks I am funny because I will try almost any food.

My family volunteers at a food bank every Saturday, which helps so many people. I know a nearby shelter accepts food donations and I am really excited to learn new Chinese recipes to bring to them. I am also excited to hold food fundraisers with the other Handstand Kids! My favorite food of all time is cookies and I can't wait to make and share the Golden Sun Almond Cookies. Yum!

13

All Kids Love ...

14

Belly Full of Beef and Broccoli

Level ////

Serves 2

Ingredients

1/2 pound top sirloin steak, cut in 1 inch strips
3 tablespoons soy sauce
1 tablespoon toasted sesame oil
1 tablespoon rice vinegar
1 tablespoon brown sugar
2 cloves minced garlic
2 tablespoons fresh ginger root, peeled and grated
2 cups broccoli florets
1 tablespoon peanut or vegetable oil
3 scallions, cut in 1-inch pieces
1/2 red bell pepper, cut in 1-inch pieces
1 teaspoon corn starch

Tools

Cutting board
Knife
Grater
Measuring cup
Measuring spoons
Wooden spoon
Slotted spoon
Medium pot
Colander or strainer
Wok or heavy large skillet
Small bowl
Re-sealable plastic bag

Alternative

Try this dish with chicken instead of beef, or make it vegetarian and use tofu!

Instructions

1. Place the sirloin strips in a large re-sealable plastic bag.

2. Add soy sauce, sesame oil, rice vinegar, brown sugar, garlic and ginger into the bag with the meat.

3. Seal the bag and place in the refrigerator for about 20 minutes.

4. Bring a medium pot of salted water to a boil. Add broccoli and cook until tender-crisp, about 2 minutes; drain in a colander and run under cold water.

5. Heat the peanut or vegetable oil in a wok or heavy skillet over high heat. Using the slotted spoon, take the marinated meat out of the bag and stir-fry in the wok for 2 minutes. Save the marinade in the bag for later.

6. When the meat is no longer pink, take it out of the wok and place it in a small bowl.

7. Add the broccoli and peppers to the wok and cook until they are slightly tender, about 3 minutes.

8. Add the scallions and cook for one minute longer.

9. Stir the cornstarch into the bag with the marinade and pour it into the wok with the vegetables.

10. Add the beef and stir-fry until the mixture boils and thickens, about 1 more minute.

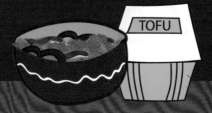

Gabby

I can't wait to bring this dish to school for lunch and share it with my friends!

16

The Great Wall of Chicken Lettuce Wraps

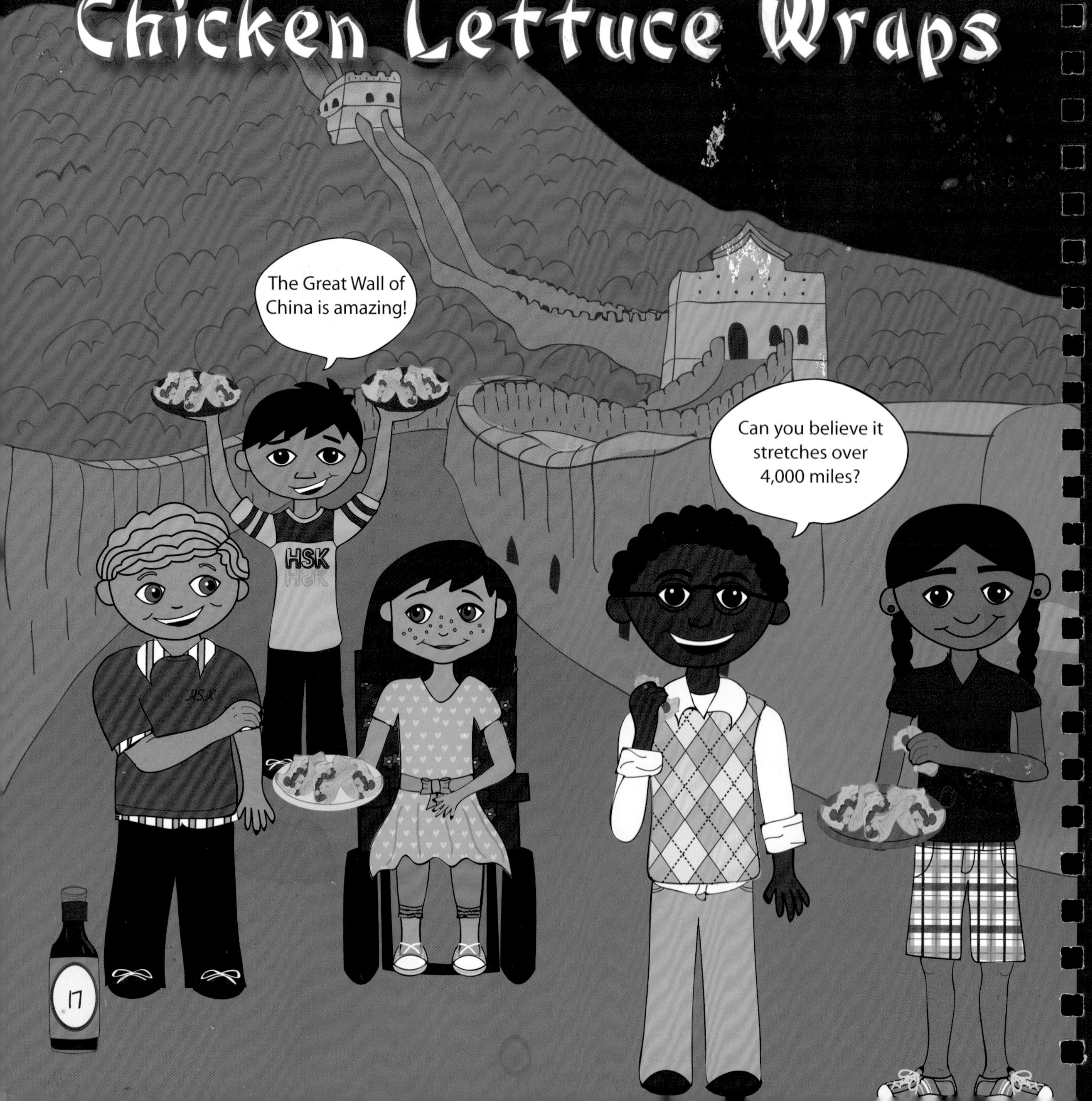

Level ///

Serves 4-6

Ingredients

1 pound boneless, skinless chicken breasts
2 tablespoons vegetable oil
Dash of salt and pepper
2 cloves minced garlic
1-inch piece of fresh ginger root, peeled and grated
3 scallions
1/2 can water chestnuts, chopped
1 cup shiitake mushrooms (about 4 medium mushrooms)
4-6 iceberg lettuce leaves
2 tablespoons soy sauce
2 tablespoons brown sugar
1/2 teaspoon rice vinegar

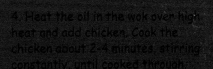

Tools

Cutting board
Knife
Measuring cups
Measuring spoons
Medium bowl
3 small bowls
Fine grater
Wok
Wooden spoon
Platter

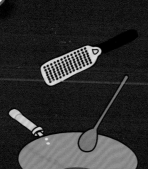

Instructions

1. Measure the soy sauce, sugar and vinegar and place into a small bowl. Stir and set aside.

2. Cut the chicken into small bite-size pieces. Sprinkle with salt and pepper. Set aside in medium bowl.

3. Chop the scallions, chestnut and mushrooms into the same size pieces as the chicken. Set aside.

4. Heat the oil in the wok over high heat and add chicken. Cook the chicken about 2-4 minutes, stirring constantly, until cooked through.

5. Stir in the garlic and ginger and cook for about 1 minute.

6. Add the chestnuts, scallions and mushrooms and cook for another 3-5 minutes.

7. Stir in the sauce and cook for 1 more minute.

8. Place chicken on a platter alongside the lettuce leave.

9. Scoop a large spoonful of the chicken into a lettuce leaf and wrap like you would a burrito.

Alternative

Use bibb or butter lettuce for a different taste and crunch.

18

I wonder how far we can walk without taking a snack break. Luckily the lettuce wraps pack up easily.

Felix

Spring-a-licious Rolls
(Baked Spring Rolls)

Level /////   Serves 4-5

Ingredients for Egg Rolls

2 ounces dried mung bean thread noodles
1 tablespoon oyster sauce
1 tablespoon chicken or vegetable broth
1/2 teaspoon sugar
1 teaspoon soy sauce
2 Napa cabbage leaves, sliced in thin strips
1 stalk celery, sliced thinly
1/2 cup fresh mung bean sprouts
1 scallion, sliced thinly
1 carrot, peeled and grated
1/2 can bamboo shoots, sliced thinly
3 shiitake mushrooms, chopped
2 tablespoons peanut oil
1/4 teaspoon toasted sesame oil
10 refrigerated spring roll wrappers
2 tablespoons water
Vegetable oil for brushing

Ingredients for Sweet and Sour Dipping Sauce

1/4 cup rice vinegar
1 tablespoon and 1 teaspoon brown sugar
1 tablespoon ketchup
1/2 tablespoon soy sauce
1 teaspoon cornstarch
4 teaspoons water

Tools

Cutting board	1 medium bowl
Knife	2 small bowls
Wok	Pastry brush
Measuring cups	Vegetable peeler
Measuring spoons	Baking sheet
Wooden spoon	Medium saucepan

Instructions for Egg Rolls

1. Preheat oven to 350 degrees.

2. Soak the dried bean thread noodles in a bowl of warm water for 10 minutes. Drain, then chop into 1 inch strands.

3. Mix the oyster sauce, chicken or vegetable broth, soy sauce, and sugar in a small bowl and set aside.

4. Heat the peanut oil in a wok or large skillet over high heat.

5. Add cabbage, celery, scallions, bamboo shoots, carrots, mushrooms, and fresh bean sprouts to the wok and stir-fry until softened (about 4 minutes).

6. Add sauce and mix thoroughly.

7. Drizzle with sesame oil and take the wok off the stove to cool. Add bean thread noodles and stir to combine.

8. Using a pastry brush, lightly coat each spring roll wrapper with oil. Turn over and place 2 tablespoonfuls of the filling in a tube shape slightly below the center of the wrapper. Be sure to leave about 1/2 inch of the edge free of filling.

9. Carefully fold up the bottom edge over the filling, then fold in the two sides to seal the mixture inside.

10. Roll the bottom up in a neat tube until it reaches the top.

11. Brush a little bit of water on the top of the wrapper to act as glue. Fold the upper edge over the tube.

12. Continue 9 more times with the remaining wrappers.

13. Place the spring rolls on a lightly oiled baking sheet and bake for about 30 minutes, until golden brown.

14. Serve with Sweet and Sour Dipping Sauce.

Instructions for Sauce

1. Place all the ingredients into a medium sauce pan.

2. Bring to a boil, stirring to thicken.

3. Once the sauce boils, carefully take it off the stove and transfer to a small serving bowl.

Alternative

Try adding shrimp, beef, or chicken to the spring roll filling!

I love using a pastry brush when I cook, it's like painting food!

Izzy

The Dynasty of Orange Chicken

Level ///

Serves 4-6

Ingredients

Instructions

1 pound boneless, skinless chicken breasts
2 teaspoons fresh ginger root, peeled and grated
4 teaspoons orange zest
1/2 cup orange juice
2 1/2 tablespoons soy sauce
1 tablespoon rice vinegar
2 teaspoon toasted sesame oil
4 teaspoons cornstarch
1 teaspoon sesame oil
1 tablespoon brown sugar
2 tablespoons chicken broth
4 tablespoons peanut oil
3 scallions, chopped
1/2 cup snow pea pods

Tools

Cutting board
Knife
Medium bowl
Small bowl
Plate
Fine grater
Wok or large skillet
Measuring cups
Measuring spoons
Wooden spoon

Alternative

Serve on top of brown or white
rice for a complete meal.

1. Cut the chicken into 1/2 inch cubes.
Place in a medium bowl.

2. To get the orange zest, lightly rub
the outside skin of the orange against
a fine grater until only the orange skin
comes off. Slice the orange in half and use the juice
too!

3. In the same bowl as the chicken, add the ginger,
2 teaspoons orange zest, 1/4 cup orange juice, 1
tablespoon soy sauce, 1 tablespoon rice vinegar,
1 teaspoon toasted sesame oil, and 2 teaspoons
cornstarch. Toss to coat the chicken well and let
marinate at room temperature for 30 minutes.

4. Wash your hands, cutting board and knife
thoroughly using hot water and soap after
handling the raw chicken.

5. While the chicken is marinating, make the sauce:
in a small bowl place 1 1/2 tablespoons soy sauce, 1
teaspoon sesame oil, 2 teaspoons orange zest, 1/4
cup orange juice, brown sugar, chicken broth, 1
teaspoon toasted sesame oil, and 2 teaspoons corn
starch. Stir and set aside for later.

6. Heat 2 tablespoons of peanut oil in a wok or
skillet over high heat until hot.

7. Drain the chicken from the marinade, place in
wok carefully, and sauté in 2 batches, about 2-3
minutes until cooked through. Remove from the
pan and place on a plate.

8. Heat 2 more tablespoons of peanut oil in a wok
or skillet over medium heat until hot.

9. Add the scallions, pea pods, chicken and sauce to the
wok and stir-fry until the sauce is hot and thickens,
about 3-5 minutes.

10. Serve immediately

Organic
Free Range
Chicken Broth

Healthy chickens, healthy people

64 Fl.o

**A grater makes it so easy to mince ginger and zest oranges!
All you have to do it rub the ginger or the orange across
the grater to shred it in tiny pieces.**

Gabby

22

Nutritious & Delicious

24

There's a Wonton in my Soup!

Ingredients for Wontons

- 1/2 pound boneless pork loin or chicken
- 1 tablespoon Hoisin sauce
- 1 teaspoon soy sauce
- 1 teaspoon chopped scallions
- 1 teaspoon fresh ginger root, peeled and grated
- 24 refrigerated wonton wrappers
- 1 teaspoon toasted sesame oil

Ingredients for the Soup

- 6 cups chicken stock
- 2 carrots
- 1 tablespoon sugar
- 1 tablespoon soy sauce
- 1/2 tablespoon fresh ginger root, peeled and grated
- 1 can bamboo shoots, drained
- 2 scallions, chopped

Tools

- Can opener
- Cutting board
- Knife
- Measuring cups
- Measuring spoons
- Fine grater
- Vegetable peeler
- Large soup pot with lid
- Wooden spoon
- Medium pot
- Large bowl
- Ladle
- Soup bowls

I made wonton soup for my aunt when she was sick and it made her feel so much better!

Marvin

Instructions for the Wontons

1. Chop the pork or chicken into very small pieces.

2. In a large bowl, mix together the pork or chicken with the Hoisin sauce, soy sauce, scallions, and ginger. Set aside to marinate for 25 minutes.

3. Bring a medium pot of water to a boil.

4. To assemble the wontons, place about 1 teaspoon of the filling at the center of a wonton wrapper. Moisten all 4 edges of the wrapper with water.

5. Pull the top corner down to the bottom, folding the wrapper over to make a triangle.
Press the edges firmly to seal the filling inside.

6. Moisten the left and right corners, bring them together over the center and press firmly to seal (so they look like a nurse's cap). Repeat until all of the wrappers are used.

7. Carefully drop the wontons into the boiling water, making sure there is enough room for them to move about freely.

8. Let the wontons boil for 5 minutes, until they rise to the top and the filling is cooked through. Remove from the pot with a slotted spoon. Place in a bowl and drizzle with a teaspoon of toasted sesame oil, gently tossing to coat each wonton. Set aside until ready to drop them into the soup.

Instructions for the Soup

1. Place the chicken stock in a large soup pot over medium high heat and bring to a boil.

2. While the stock is heating up, peel and slice the carrots into thin rounds and add to the pot. Stir in the sugar and soy sauce.

3. Add the ginger and bamboo shoots to the pot.

4. Once the pot is boiling, drop in the cooked wontons and cook for another 5 minutes.

5. Ladle soup and wontons into each bowl, and sprinkle chopped scallions on top for garnish.

Alternative

TOFU

For a vegetarian soup, try using tofu instead of meat for the wonton filling and use vegetable stock instead of chicken stock. Yum Yum!

26

Level //

Serves 4-6

Ingredients for the Peanut Dressing

1/3 cup peanut butter
1 1/2 teaspoons toasted sesame oil
2 teaspoons fresh ginger root, peeled and grated
2 teaspoons honey
1 tablespoon rice vinegar
2 teaspoons soy sauce
4 tablespoons water
1 tablespoon chopped scallions

Ingredients for the Salad

1/2 head Napa cabbage
1/2 head Romaine lettuce
2 carrots
1/4 pound fresh snow peas
2 cups shredded cooked chicken
1/4 cup mint leaves, chopped finely
1/2 cup roasted peanuts

Tools

Cutting Board
Knife
Measuring cups
Measuring spoons
Whisk
Vegetable peeler
Medium bowl
Large serving bowl
Re-sealable plastic bag
Rolling pin

Instructions for the Dressing

1. Measure all the ingredients into a medium bowl and whisk until fully incorporated.

Instructions for the Salad

1. Shred the cabbage and lettuce into thin strips. Place in a large serving bowl.

2. Peel and shred the carrots and place on top of the lettuce mixture.

3. Julianne the snow pea into thin strips and add to the bowl.

4. Spoon in a few tablespoons of the dressing and toss everything until well coated.

5. Top with the shredded chicken.

6. Sprinkle the chopped mint leaves on top of salad.

7. Crush the peanuts in a sealed plastic bag by using a rolling pin and sprinkle over salad.

Alternative

For a heartier meal, add cooked Chinese noodles to the salad!

The extra dressing can be used as a yummy dipping sauce or for a meat marinade.

28

Julienne means to cut into very thin strips.

Ari

A Feast Fit for Buddha
(Buddha's Feast Vegetables with Tofu)

Level ///

Serves 3-4

Ingredients

2 tablespoons soy sauce
1 tablespoon toasted sesame oil
1/4 cup vegetable or chicken stock
1 tablespoon corn starch
1 tablespoon fresh ginger root, peeled and grated
4 ounces firm tofu
2 carrots
1 zucchini
2 medium shiitake mushrooms
3 ounces sugar snap peas
2 heads baby bok choy
2 scallions
1 clove garlic, minced
1/2 can (4 ounces) sliced water chestnuts, drained
1 tablespoon peanut oil

Tools

Cutting board
Knife
Fine grater
Measuring cups
Measuring spoons
Vegetable peeler
Medium bowl
Small bowl
Wooden spoon
Wok or large skillet

Alternative

You can use any of your favorite vegetables in this dish. Try using shrimp, chicken, or beef instead of tofu!

Instructions

1. In a small bowl, whisk together soy sauce, sesame oil, stock, corn starch and ginger.

2. Cut tofu into ½ inch cubes. Place into soy sauce mixture. Let marinate while you prepare the other ingredients.

3. Peel and slice the carrots into rounds about ¼ inch thick.

4. Slice the zucchini in half lengthwise then cut into half circles about ¼ inch thick.

5. Clean the shiitake mushrooms gently with a damp towel. Remove the stem and cut into slices about ¼ inch thick.

6. Slice each snap pea in half.

7. Quarter the baby bok choy then cut each piece in half.

8. Chop the scallions into small pieces.

9. Now drain the tofu and save the remaining sauce in a small bowl for later.

10. Heat 1 tablespoon peanut oil into a wok or large skillet over medium heat. Add the carrots, zucchini and mushrooms. Cook for 4 minutes, stirring frequently.

11. Add the snap peas, bok choy, scallions, garlic, water chestnuts and tofu. Cook for 4-6 minutes, stirring frequently. Add the reserved sauce and stir until sauce thickens, about 1-2 minutes.

12. Serve immediately over a bowl of brown rice.

I once made Buddha s feast with 15 vegetables. It was awesome!

Izzy

30

Level ///

Ingredients

12 ounces firm tofu
4 tablespoons peanut or vegetable oil
1 stalk celery, diced
1/2 cup diced carrots
1/2 red bell pepper, diced
1/2 yellow onion, diced
1 cup snow peas, halved
1/2 cup chopped water chestnuts
5 scallions, cut in 1/2-inch pieces
3 cloves minced garlic
1/2 cup roasted peanuts
1/4 cup soy sauce
2 tablespoons toasted sesame oil
1 tablespoon sugar
1 teaspoon Hoisin sauce
2 tablespoons rice vinegar
1 tablespoon cornstarch mixed with 2 tablespoons water

Tools

Cutting board
Knife
2 plates
Measuring cups
Measuring spoons
Wooden spoon
Wok or large skillet
Small bowl

Instructions

1. Take the tofu out of the container and drain off the excess water. Wrap several paper towels around the tofu and place on a plate. Position another plate on top of the tofu and place a heavy object, like a can of soup, on the plate to use as a weight. Let sit for 15 minutes, pouring off any water that collects on the plate. Pat the tofu dry and cut into bite-size cubes.

2. Heat 2 tablespoons of the oil in the wok or large heavy skillet over medium-high heat and add the tofu.

3. Fry the tofu, turning until each side is golden brown. Remove from the pan and drain on a paper towel. Set aside.

4. To make the sauce, mix together soy sauce, toasted sesame oil, sugar, Hoisin sauce, rice vinegar and corn starch in a small bowl and set aside so the flavors mingle.

5. Heat the remaining 2 tablespoon of oil in a wok or large skillet over medium-high heat.

6. Add the celery, carrots, peppers and yellow onions and cook, stirring often, until softened (about 5 minutes).

7. Add the snow peas, water chestnuts, scallions and garlic and cook for another 2 to 3 minutes.

8. Add the tofu, sauce and peanuts. Stir until heated through and thickened, about 1 more minute.

Alternative

This dish would also taste delicious with beef or shrimp instead of tofu.

I love eating tofu after karate practice. It gives me energy so I can practice even more!
Felix

32

33

Chinese-ify My...

34

Rice into Shrimp Fried Rice

Level ////

Ingredients

4 tablespoons peanut oil
½ pound medium shrimp, shelled and de-veined
2 eggs, beaten with 1 teaspoon sesame oil
3 scallions, chopped
2 cloves garlic, minced
1 teaspoon fresh ginger root, peeled and grated
2 carrots, peeled and diced
12 ounces (1 ½ cups) cooked long grain white rice
3 ounces fresh bean sprouts
3 tablespoons soy sauce

Organic Sesame Oil 10 FL OZ

Organic White Rice 500 g

Instructions

1. Cook rice according to directions on the package or use leftover cooked rice.

2. Heat 2 tablespoons of the peanut oil in a wok or large skillet over high heat. Swirl the pan to coat the wok with oil.

3. Add the shrimp and stir-fry just until pink, about 2 minutes. Remove shrimp from the pan and set aside in a small bowl.

4. Add eggs to the wok and scramble until cooked. Remove from the pan, break into bite-size pieces, and set aside with the shrimp.

5. Wipe the wok clean, return it to the heat and add the remaining 2 tablespoons of peanut oil. Reduce heat to medium-high.

6. Add the scallions, garlic, ginger and carrots and stir-fry for 1 minute.

7. Stir in the rice, bean sprouts, soy sauce, egg and shrimp. Continue cooking for another 3 minutes until everything is heated through, stirring frequently so the rice doesn't stick to the pan.

8. Serve immediately.

Tools

Cutting board
Knife
Measuring cups
Measuring spoons
Small bowl
Wok or large skillet
Wooden spoon

Alternative

Organic Brown Rice

Try brown rice instead of white rice to make this dish super healthy and yummy!

36

Gabby

Cooking with a wok is the coolest! Because it's so big, you can cook food in it really fast, but make sure to stir everything often!

Level //

Ingredients

1 ball (16 ounces) prepared pizza dough
1 tablespoon olive oil
1/4 cup Hoisin sauce
2 cups shredded cooked rotisserie chicken
2 scallions, sliced, green and light green parts only
1/4 red bell pepper, sliced in thin strips
1/2 can water chestnuts, drained and chopped
2 cups grated mozzarella cheese
1/2 cup cilantro, chopped
1/2 cup flour for workspace

Tools

Cutting board
Knife
Measuring cups
Measuring spoons
Small bowls
Cheese grater
Large spatula
Pizza stone or baking sheet
Rolling pin (optional)
Pizza cutter (optional)

Alternative

Make this pizza vegetarian by leaving out the chicken. Feel free to experiment with different types of veggies, too!

Instructions

1. Preheat oven to 450 degrees or according to cooking instructions on the package. Insert pizza stone to preheat, if using.

2. Let the dough come to room temperature. Cut dough into four even pieces and rub them with olive oil.

3. Sprinkle your workspace with flour so the dough doesn't stick to the surface. Place a ball of dough in the middle of the workspace and roll it with a rolling pin or spread it, pulling very gently at the edges with your hands, into a 1/4-inch circle or rectangle.

4. Spread Hoisin sauce over the surface of the dough, leaving the edges bare to create a nice crust.

5. Place a thin layer of cheese over the sauce.

6. Spread chicken, scallions, bell peppers and water chestnuts over the cheese.

7. Follow with another thin layer of cheese on top.

8. Repeat this process with the other three pieces of dough.

9. Carefully transfer pizzas onto the pizza stone or lightly oiled baking sheet and bake for 8-10 minutes or until the dough is golden brown and the cheese is bubbly.

10. Carefully remove from the pizza stone or baking sheet using a large spatula and set on a plate to cool slightly.

11. Sprinkle the pizzas with chopped cilantro and slice using a pizza cutter or knife. Serve immediately.

38

My family makes this pizza with lots of veggies and tofu. It's the best!

Felix

Level ////   Serves 4

Ingredients

8 ounces dried Chinese yakisoba noodles
1/2 cup chicken or vegetable broth
1 tablespoon toasted sesame oil
1 teaspoon brown sugar
1 teaspoon corn starch
2 teaspoons soy sauce
1/2 small yellow onion
2 carrots
2 stalks celery
2 medium shitake mushrooms
2 heads baby bok choy
2 scallions
1/2 can sliced water chestnuts, drained
2 tablespoons peanut oil

Tools

Large pot
Colander
Measuring cups
Measuring spoons
Whisk
Small bowl
Knife
Cutting board
Wok or large nonstick skillet
Wooden spoon

Alternative

Try experimenting with different types
of noodles and veggies.

Instructions

1. Boil the noodles according to package directions. Drain in a colander in the sink and rinse under cold running water for 15 seconds. Shake off excess water. Set aside.

2. Whisk together the broth, sesame oil, sugar, corn starch and soy sauce into a small bowl. Set aside.

3. Slice the onion into thin half moons.

4. Peel the carrots and cut into thin rounds.

5. Cut the celery stalks into thin slices.

6. Clean the shitake mushrooms gently with a damp towel. Remove the stem and slice thinly.

7. Quarter the baby bok choy, then slice each quarter in half.

8. Cut the scallions crosswise into 1/2-inch thick pieces.

9. Heat peanut oil into a wok or large skillet over high heat.

10. Add the onions, carrots, celery and mushrooms and stir-fry for about 2 minutes.

11. Add the bok choy, scallions, and chestnuts. Cook for 3 minutes, stirring frequently.

12. Pour in the sauce, bring to a boil, and stir.

13. Add the noodles and stir to coat with the sauce and heat through. Serve immediately.

40

Marvin

My mom told me a story about the world's longest noodle - it was 136 miles long. That would take a long time to eat!

Popcorn into Chinese Popcorn

Level

Ingredients

1/2 cup popcorn kernels or 1 bag of plain microwave popcorn
2 tablespoons butter
1 tablespoon toasted sesame oil
2 teaspoons soy sauce
2 tablespoons black sesame seeds

Tools

Measuring cup
Measuring spoons
Whisk
Small bowl
2 paper lunch bags
2 oven mitts

Alternative

To add a little spice, sprinkle some red chili pepper flakes into the butter mixture. Start with a very tiny amount to make sure it is not too spicy.

Instructions

1. In the microwave, heat the butter for 20 seconds or until melted.

2. Whisk the sesame oil, soy sauce and sesame seeds into the butter.

3. Pop the popcorn in a popcorn machine or microwave.

4. Wearing oven mitts, place the popped kernels in the brown lunch bags. Pour the butter mixture evenly over the popcorn and shake the bag for 30 seconds.

5. Enjoy!

When we watch movies at home I love to make Chinese popcorn for everyone to share.

Izzy

42

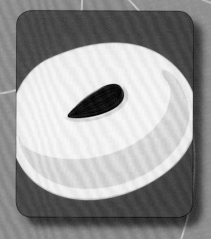

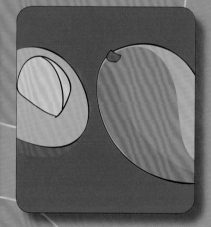

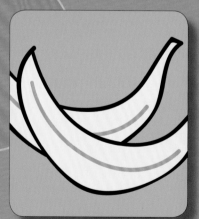

43

Save Room For...

44

The Emperor's Favorite Treat, Chocolate Noodle Clusters

Level /

Serves 8-10

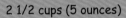

Ingredients

2 cups (12 ounce bag) semi-sweet chocolate chips

2 tablespoons (1 ounce) unsalted butter

2 1/2 cups (5 ounces)

Chinese chow mein noodles, broken into 1-inch pieces

1 1/4 cups (5 ounces) salted peanuts

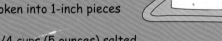

Instructions

1. Line a baking sheet with wax paper, parchment paper, or aluminum foil.

2. Melt the chocolate chips and butter together in a microwave-safe bowl in a microwave oven, stirring every 30 seconds. Heat just until the chocolate is melted and the mixture is smooth.

3. In a large mixing bowl, toss the noodles and peanuts together. Pour the melted chocolate mixture over them and stir. Use a rubber spatula to coat the noodles and nuts with chocolate quickly before the chocolate hardens.

4. Use 2 soup spoons to scoop up spoonfuls of the mixture and place on the prepared baking sheet. Set the baking sheet in a cool place or refrigerate for 15 minutes until the chocolate hardens.

5. The clusters can be stored in an airtight container at room temperature for up to 1 month.

Tools

Measuring cups
Medium microwaveable bowl
Large mixing bowl
Rubber spatula
Nonstick baking sheet
2 soup spoons

Alternative

Try using different types of nuts. You can also leave out the nuts and just use the chow mein noodles!

Marvin

These are so delicious and easy to make. I brought them for my school holiday party last year and everybody wanted to know how to make them.

46

Golden Sun Almond Cookies

Level ///

Serves 6-8

Ingredients

1 cup flour

1/4 teaspoon salt

1/4 teaspoon baking soda

1/2 cup butter, softened at room temperature

1/2 cup sugar

1 teaspoon almond extract

1 egg

20 whole almonds

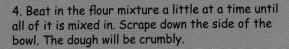

Tools

Measuring cups
Measuring spoons
Medium mixing bowl
Large mixing bowl
Small bowl
Electric hand mixer
Sifter or fine mesh sieve
Rubber spatula
Nonstick baking sheet
Pastry brush
Spatula

Instructions

1. Preheat oven to 325 degrees.

2. In a medium mixing bowl, sift together flour, baking soda and salt. Set aside.

3. In a large mixing bowl, use an electric mixer to beat the butter until creamy. Beat in the sugar and almond extract. Scrape down the sides of the bowl with a rubber spatula.

4. Beat in the flour mixture a little at a time until all of it is mixed in. Scrape down the side of the bowl. The dough will be crumbly.

5. Gently roll the dough into 1-inch balls. Place the balls on an ungreased baking sheet 2 inches apart. Carefully press down with the palm of your hand to flatten the balls slightly.

6. In a small bowl, beat the egg and use a pastry brush to brush each cookie with the egg. Place a whole almond in the center of each cookie.

7. Bake for 15-18 minutes, or until lightly golden brown. Remove the baking sheet from the oven. Then use the spatula to remove the cookies from the baking sheet onto a wire rack.

8. Allow them to cool slightly. Store leftover cookies in an airtight container, if there are any!

Alternative

When making these cookies for friends with nut allergies, leave out the almonds and try a piece of chocolate or dried fruit instead.

The almond cookies that my mom and I make are even better than the ones we eat in Chinese restaurants.

Felix

Banana-rama Spring Rolls

Level ///

Ingredients

2 tablespoons butter
2 large bananas
8 spring roll wrappers
1/2 cup brown sugar
Powdered sugar

Brown Sugar

Rice Paper

Net Weight 17.6 oz.

Tools

Knife
Cutting board
Medium mixing bowl
Measuring cups
Measuring spoons
Small microwave-safe bowl
Pastry brush
Nonstick baking sheet
Parchment paper
Spatula

Instructions

1. Preheat oven to 375 degrees. Line a baking sheet with parchment paper.

2. In the microwave, heat the butter in a small, microwave-safe bowl for 20 seconds or until melted.

3. Peel the bananas and cut them lengthwise. Then slice each one in half. You should have 8 pieces total. Place them in the medium mixing bowl.

4. Toss the bananas with brown sugar and set aside.

5. Lay out a spring roll wrapper on your cutting board. Brush both sides with melted butter using your pastry brush.

6. Place a piece of banana diagonally across the corner of a wrapper. Roll from that corner to the center of the wrapper, then fold over the two side corners and continue rolling until you have a nice sealed package.

7. Repeat with the remaining banana pieces and wrappers.

8. Place the finished rolls onto the baking sheet and bake for 12-15 minutes. The bottom of the rolls will brown, however, the tops may not.

9. Carefully take the baking sheet out of the oven and let cool for 5 minutes.

10. Place the rolls on a serving plate using a spatula and sprinkle with powdered sugar. Enjoy!

Alternative

CHOCOLATE SAUCE

Drizzle the rolls with chocolate sauce before serving for an extra treat.

50

Making banana spring rolls is like doing an art project. I love carefully rolling them up into packages. They look and taste amazing!

Felix

Year of the Monkey Mango Smoothies

Ingredients

6 ounces silken tofu, drained

1 medium banana, peeled and cut in half

1 mango

1/4-inch piece fresh ginger root, peeled and grated (optional)

2/3 cup soy milk

1 tablespoon honey

4 ice cubes

Good Foods
Plain Yogurt

Silken Tofu

Tools

Cutting board
Knife
Measuring cups
Measuring spoons
Fine grater
Blender
Tall drinking glasses

Alternative

Add 2/3 cup plain yogurt if tofu is not available.

Instructions

1. Cut the mango by placing the mango with one flat side resting on the cutting board. Slice the mango lengthwise along the flat side next to the seed. Turn mango over and repeat on the other side. You will have 2 halves of the mango with pulp inside. Carefully cut lengthwise through the mango pulp down to the skin, being careful not to cut through the skin. Turn sideways and cut lengthwise again until you have a cross-hatch pattern. Turn the mango inside out using your thumbs to press the pulp outwards. Carefully slice out the diced pulp by cutting between the cubed mango pulp and the skin. Discard the skin and seed.

2. Place banana, mango, tofu, soy milk, and ginger, if using, into the blender. Blend on medium speed for 30 seconds.

3. Add the honey and ice cubes and blend again until smooth.

4. Pour into 2 frosty tall drinking glasses. Enjoy!

This is my favorite drink to make during the summer. I can have it for breakfast or drink it all day long. Yum!

Gabby

52